HUMAN
TRAFFICKING

Essential Issues

HUMAN

TRAFFICKING

BY COURTNEY FARRELL

Content Consultant
Mark Hoerrner
Executive Board Member, Georgia Rescue and Restore
Founder, Ethical Living Inc.

ABDO
Publishing Company

CREDITS

Published by ABDO Publishing Company, 8000 West 78th Street, Edina, Minnesota 55439. Copyright © 2011 by Abdo Consulting Group, Inc. International copyrights reserved in all countries. No part of this book may be reproduced in any form without written permission from the publisher. The Essential Library™ is a trademark and logo of ABDO Publishing Company.

Printed in the United States of America,
North Mankato, Minnesota
112010
012011

 THIS BOOK CONTAINS AT LEAST 10% RECYCLED MATERIALS.

Editor: Amy Van Zee
Copy Editor: David Johnstone
Interior Design and Production: Becky Daum
Cover Design: Marie Tupy

Library of Congress Cataloging-in-Publication Data
Farrell, Courtney.
  Human trafficking / by Courtney Farrell.
     p. cm.
  Includes bibliographical references.
  ISBN 978-1-61714-773-9
     1. Human trafficking--Juvenile literature. 2. Child trafficking--Juvenile literature. I. Title.
  HQ281.F37 2011
  364.15--dc22

                          2010044267

TABLE OF CONTENTS

Chapter 1	Trafficking Is Modern Slavery	6
Chapter 2	Debt Slavery in South Asia	18
Chapter 3	Kids for Sale in the Middle East	28
Chapter 4	Trafficking of Women	38
Chapter 5	Child Trafficking in Africa	46
Chapter 6	Central American Babies for Sale	56
Chapter 7	There Is Still Slavery in America	66
Chapter 8	The Impact of Trafficking on Survivors	76
Chapter 9	Solving the Problem	86
Timeline		96
Essential Facts		100
Glossary		102
Additional Resources		104
Source Notes		106
Index		110
About the Author		112

Villagers taken as slaves by the Communist Party of Nepal worked on a road in July 2005. Some slaves were as young as six.

Trafficking Is Modern Slavery

ine-year-old Williathe Narcisse was a slave in Haiti before she arrived in the southern United States to work for her new owners there. In the United States, she cleaned house for her mistress, worked in her master's business, and was abused sexually by their adult son. If she dared complain about her treatment, she was whipped until she bled. Before the United States made slavery illegal in 1865, countless other black girls experienced similar abuse. What makes this story so shocking is not that it happened at all, but that it happened in 1996.

Williathe was a *restavèk*—a Haitian child kept in involuntary servitude. In Haiti, one out of every ten children between the ages of 12 and 15 is a restavèk. This system is a normal part of life in the nation. Poor rural families often send their children to live with wealthier families in cities. The typical agreement is for the child to do chores in exchange for food, clothing, and schooling. However, most restavèks in Haiti do not attend school. They have too much work to do. Many homes there have no running water, so restavèks haul water

Slavery Is Not Rare

No one knows exactly how many slaves there are in the world. Slaves are kept hidden and are not counted in censuses, so statistics can be difficult to determine. However, experts estimate there are approximately 27 million people enslaved today out of a total world population of almost 7 billion. Some estimates are as high as 60 million.

in buckets. Washing machines are rare, so laundry and dishes are done by hand. In Haiti, 16-hour workdays are not unusual for restavèks, and whipping is a socially acceptable means for punishing them. When Williathe got the chance to go to Florida, she thought it meant a better life—but she was wrong.

Williathe's new owners, Marie and Willy Pompee, hired a human smuggler who obtained a false passport for the girl. The smuggler, an older black woman who posed as the child's mother, delivered Williathe to Miami. There, the child worked constantly, slept on a mattress on the basement floor, and did not get enough to eat. When she displeased her owners, they whipped her hard enough to leave scars. Willy Jr., the couple's 18-year-old son, regularly raped her. Luckily for Williathe, US law requires children to attend school. Marie did not want to be caught violating the law, so she enrolled the girl in public school.

Williathe had trouble keeping up with her class. Her captors did not give her time to do homework, and they made her work every evening and weekend. In 1999, three years after arriving in the United States, she went to school in terrible pain. A staff member gently took her aside, and the truth came out. The child was torn and bleeding from frequent rapes, and she was suffering from a sexually transmitted infection (STI).

Although Willy and his son fled the country, Marie was convicted of harboring an illegal alien. She was sentenced to six months in prison because she claimed that she knew nothing of the sexual abuse. "I'm kind of mad she didn't pay for what she did," Williathe said. "But then again, her going to jail for more years can't take my pain away."[1]

To save Williathe the trauma of

Slavery in America

Slaves first came to America around the year 1619, when a Dutch ship arrived at the Virginia colony in Jamestown with approximately 20 African slaves. The Africans had endured a harrowing journey. They were originally captured by Portuguese slavers in southwest Africa and crowded into the hold of a ship called the *San Juan Bautista*. During its passage, the *San Juan Bautista* came under attack by two British pirate ships flying the Dutch flag. The pirates won the battle, but they did not free the slaves. Instead, they stole them from the Portuguese and split them up between their two ships. They later traded some of the slaves to the colonists for food. In a letter, colonist John Rolfe wrote that the ship "brought not any thing but 20 and odd Negroes, [which] the Governor and Cape Marchant bought for [food] . . . at the best and [easiest] rate they could."[2]

Some of these early slaves were eventually freed. But by the time the Civil War began in 1861, there were approximately 4 million slaves in the American South. President Abraham Lincoln's Emancipation Proclamation declared them free in 1862, but most were not actually freed until 1865, when the Thirteenth Amendment to the US Constitution was passed.

appearing in court, the prosecutor chose not to seek an indictment on charges of involuntary servitude. The judge placed her in foster care, where she grew up. Although she had psychological difficulties as a result of her trauma, Williathe is largely recovered today. At last report, she was attending college.

What Is a Slave?

People sometimes disagree about what constitutes slavery. Was Williathe a slave or an abused child with too many chores?

The term *involuntary servitude* is sometimes used instead of *slavery*, but the idea is much the same. Involuntary servitude is a situation in which a person works against his or her will for the profit of another individual and cannot leave. This definition does seem to fit Williathe's situation, but it was never proven in court.

The difference between unfair working conditions and involuntary servitude is not always clear. For example, if a construction company underpays its workers and puts them in substandard housing, is that slavery? What if the supervisors took workers' passports, making it hard for them to leave or find other jobs? What if they "paid" their workers only with food? Are the workers slaves, or are they mistreated employees? Would it make a difference if the workers were brought into the country illegally or if they were lured there with false promises? To draft laws banning human trafficking, national and international leaders had to wrestle with questions such as these.

Human trafficking is often misunderstood to mean smuggling people across borders illegally. It involves much more than that. Traffickers often move their captives, but they can be guilty even without doing so. Trafficking victims are people who are exploited through force, fraud, or coercion—even within the victim's own country. The traffickers profit from the efforts of their victims, who generally fall into one of two categories: sexual slavery or forced labor.

Why People Are Trafficked

Traffickers are motivated by money. It is difficult to estimate how much money human trafficking generates each year, but the estimate is upward of $30 billion. In the United States, a pimp can make as much as $250,000 per year from a single trafficked sex slave. Trafficking victims who become household servants are less profitable, but they do save their owners the money that would have been spent on wages.

Force, Fraud, and Coercion

Some trafficking victims are captured and kept by force. Some are imprisoned in chains or under guard, but there are other kinds of force as well. For example, pimps are people, usually men, who own sex slaves and find business for them. Pimps often use beatings and gang rapes to keep their sex slaves too frightened to attempt escape, even though the slaves may move freely about the streets.

Fraud is intentional deception resulting in injury to another person. Traffickers commit fraud when they lie to lure their victims into going along willingly. Common promises include too good to be true deals offering high wages, easy work, and nice housing. Another type of fraud is that of pretended affection. This is called the "loverboy" approach, because young, handsome traffickers charm vulnerable girls into trusting them. The girl believes she is in a loving relationship but finds out otherwise when the boyfriend sells her into prostitution.

When a trafficker forces a victim to obey through fear, intimidation, or threats, this is known as coercion. Some traffickers never physically abuse their victims but use psychological tactics instead. They might threaten their victims' families or lie to

Five-year-old Priyanka Sharma scavenges for used plastic containers to sell in New Delhi, India. Overpopulation and poverty have contributed to human trafficking in Southeast Asia.

them, exaggerating the dangers of the outside world. Undocumented immigrants are especially susceptible to this approach because traffickers can threaten them with deportation if they go to the authorities.

Poverty Is a Risk Factor for Trafficking

A 2009 study by Dr. Emmanuel Saez of the University of California—Berkeley demonstrated what many people intuitively know: the rich are getting richer, while the poor are getting poorer. As the human population increases, competition for remaining resources naturally intensifies. The result is widespread poverty and desperation, especially in the developing world. Desperate people are easy to identify, and traffickers flock to these areas to take advantage of them. Not surprisingly, badly overpopulated regions such as India and Southeast Asia are also rife with human traffickers. In a twisted example of the economics of supply and demand, the price of a life tends to be lowest where overcrowding is worst.

In 1850, an African slave was a huge investment, costing the

Exploitation of Illegal Immigrants

On August 2, 1995, 72 Thai workers were freed from a Los Angeles, California, sweatshop, where they sewed clothing for 17 hours per day. They made less than $1 per hour and slept on rodent- and cockroach-infested floors. Razor wire enclosed the factory to prevent workers from escaping. "I never thought I could get out of there," said Maliwan Radonphon, a young seamstress.[3] In 1996, the workers won a $4 million lawsuit against the sweatshop owners.

equivalent of $40,000 in today's dollars. The price alone motivated slaveholders to provide at least minimal care for their slaves—after all, they needed to protect their investment. Today, although prices vary, a slave costs relatively little. In very poor countries such as Haiti, children can be purchased for as little as $50. In some Asian countries such as Thailand, they can be bought for just a few dollars. Slave owners who are concerned only with money can replace workers for less than it would cost to provide them with proper food or medical care.

"Legal slaves were property, and watched over because they were an asset," says Marcelo Campos, head of the antislavery program at Brazil's Ministry of Labor. "They had food and shelter because the owner needed to make sure they stayed alive. Today's slave is not a concern (to the landowner). He uses them as an

Slave Labor in the Amazon

A 2009 report by the International Labour Conference estimated that there are 33,000 forced laborers in Amazon jungle camps. Camp bosses exploit both people and the environment, destroying the forest by gold mining and logging. "It's hard to think of worse exploitation than what we went through," says Geyner Pizango, an unpaid Peruvian worker who was arrested in Brazil for illegal logging and deported. "The Brazilians called us modern slaves, and they were right. We were sent into the jungle, imprisoned for trying to make an honest wage and treated like animals."[4]

absolutely temporary item, like a disposable razor."[5] In the case of human trafficking, environmental, economic, and social problems are all inescapably intertwined. ⸺

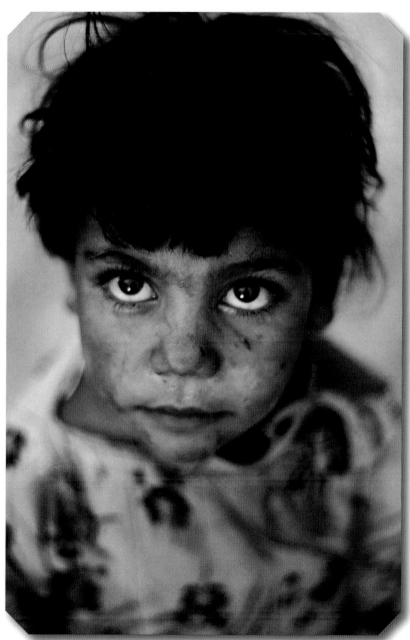

In April 2010, Rukhia Khan resided in a refugee camp in Kabul, Afghanistan. Refugees are especially vulnerable to human trafficking.

Cambodian men who were victims of human traffickers prepare to return to their families after being rescued by human rights workers in 1997.

Debt Slavery in South Asia

The system of debt bondage is sometimes called debt slavery because employers exploit generations of workers for little or no pay. Debt bondage is common in India, Pakistan, Nepal, and other nations in South Asia, but it has spread all over the world. A family's descent into slavery begins when someone—usually the father—borrows money from a landlord or an employer. Unable to repay the debt, the borrower agrees to pay off the loan with his or her labor. The borrower works hard, but the debt is never paid off, because employers charge high rates of interest on the loans. Fines and charges for expenses such as clothing, tools, housing, medical care, weddings, and funerals are added to the debt. Because so many bonded laborers are illiterate, individuals often do not know exactly how much money they owe, or how the interest on the loan is calculated. Some bonded laborers sell themselves and their families into slavery for debts as small as ten dollars.

Employers provide bonded laborers with rudimentary housing such as mud and straw huts. The employers give them barely enough

Pakistani Law Prohibits Debt Bondage

In 1992, Pakistan passed the Bonded Labor System Abolition Act, making the practice of debt slavery illegal. Follow-up legislation in 1995—the Bonded Labor System Abolition Rules—established committees to find, rescue, and rehabilitate bonded laborers.

In 2002, the Prevention and Control of Human Trafficking Ordinance outlined punishment for those involved in human trafficking and the exploitation of people under the age of 18. Punishment for those found guilty of exploiting children for sexual, abusive, or entertainment purposes is seven to 14 years in prison. This punishment also applies to parents guilty of exploiting or trafficking their own children.

food to keep them alive. Laborers usually live on or near their work sites, where they marry and raise their children. Children of bonded laborers rarely go to school, and most begin working when they are as young as four years old. When the parents die, the children inherit the family's debts. Three generations or more of bonded laborers might belong to their employers, who likewise pass on their own businesses from father to son.

Bonded labor is illegal in India, Nepal, and Pakistan, but the practice is still common in these nations. Officials are often corrupt, and employers can easily bribe them to overlook infractions. Bonded labor is frequently seen in agricultural work, quarries, and in factories that produce bricks and handwoven carpets. However, it is used in other businesses as well. Western tourists do not always realize it, but some workers in Asian hotels and restaurants might be slaves.

CHILD LABOR IN CARPET FACTORIES

Hand-knotted Persian carpets are some of the most beautiful in the world, but child slaves make many of them. In South Asia, up to 90 percent of the employees of carpet factories are children between the ages of four and 14. Carpet masters constantly recruit new labor, mostly targeting boys between seven and ten years old. "They make ideal employees," says a Pakistani carpet master named Sadique. "Boys at this stage of development are at the peak of their dexterity and endurance, and they're wonderfully obedient—they'd work around the clock if I asked them."[1]

The children are not really as willing as Sadique makes them sound. The younger ones will wander away from their looms, so carpet masters chain them there. Children who cry

Iqbal's Escape from the Carpet Factory

Iqbal Masih was a Pakistani boy who was sold into slavery by his father when he was four years old. Iqbal's father was a drug addict who abandoned the family, but he returned to see his oldest son get married. It is Pakistani tradition for the father to pay for the wedding, but Mr. Masih had no money. He took a $12 loan from the owner of a carpet factory, promising that little Iqbal would work off the debt. Inayat, Iqbal's mother, could do nothing about the agreement because women in Pakistan have few rights. When Iqbal was ten years old, he slipped away from the factory and attended a Bonded Labor Liberation Front (BLLF) rally. There he learned that bonded labor was illegal, and he broke out of bondage.

Iqbal began to work with the BLLF to free other child slaves too. He received death threats from men in the carpet industry, but he did not stop. When he was 12 years old, the BLLF took him on a worldwide tour to speak out against child slavery. Iqbal was murdered on April 16, 1995, when he returned to Pakistan. The killer was never caught, but many people believe it was a hit man hired by the carpet industry.

or work too slowly are punished by being beaten with carpet tools. Masters underfeed children to keep them small, claiming that tiny fingers do the best weaving.

Underfeeding improves profits, because food costs money. The primary motive for using child labor is savings. "I hire them first and foremost because they're economical," Sadique explains. "For what I'd pay one second-class adult weaver I can get three boys, sometimes four, who can produce first-class rugs in no time."[2]

Carpet masters make a profit, but many of their workers end up dying young. Sunlight fades wool, so factories are kept dark and stuffy. Children's backs become permanently hunched from crouching over looms for 16 hours a day. Exhausted young weavers sometimes lose focus and cut themselves with their sharp tools. They contract lung diseases from inhaling the wool fibers, but illness is no excuse for missing work. If these young workers die, more can be readily found.

Sadique persuasively recruits more workers. "I've admired your boy for several months," Sadique says to Mirza, the ragged father of a seven-year-old. "Nadeem is bright and ambitious. He will learn far

Twelve-year-old Mohammad Reza labored in a small Afghan carpet workshop in 2004.

more practical skills in six months at the loom than he would in six years of school. He will be taught by experienced craftsmen, and his pay will rise as his skills improve. Have no doubt, your son will be thankful for the opportunity you have given him, and the Lord will bless you for looking so well after your own."[3]

Sadique offers the family approximately $150 for five years of Nadeem's labor, and Nadeem is not consulted about the deal. Fees for the child's equipment, food, and training will be deducted, but the family will not discover that until later. Nadeem's desperately poor parents haggle a bit on the price, but in the end, another young slave will enter the carpet factory.

Caste Discrimination

The Hindu caste system directly contributes to the problem of debt slavery. This system is a hierarchy of social classes that extends throughout South Asia, with some castes outranking others. Caste discrimination has been outlawed, but the problem persists.

Castes once contributed to their villages in specific ways by practicing certain professions or performing specific services. The Brahman caste was historically made up of priests and scholars, while the Kshatriya caste included warriors, kings, and landowners. Individuals born into higher castes such as these are presumed to have good karma from virtuous deeds in past lives. Karma is the idea that a person's actions during past lives affect their present lives. Modern individuals in higher castes are often, but not always, wealthier and better educated than those from lower castes. Castes are hereditary, so children are born with the same social status as their parents. This perpetuates a cycle of economic disparity.

The lower castes are now called *scheduled castes*. The vast majority of bonded laborers throughout South Asia come from scheduled castes. Among them are the lowest-ranking members of Hindu society, formerly called untouchables. *Untouchable* is a term that is no longer used in polite company. It has been replaced with the term *dalit*, a name that means "downtrodden." Dalits were traditionally forced to perform the dirtiest jobs, such as hauling manure or cleaning latrines.

In rural villages, dalits who refuse to put up with abuse face brutal retaliation from higher castes. Insubordinate dalits have been boycotted, meaning that fellow villagers block them from access to land, markets, and jobs. With no

Religion Influences the Bonded Labor System

Religious teachings of tolerance can inadvertently perpetuate injustice if those beliefs prevent oppressed workers from demanding their rights. Hindus believe in reincarnation and the concept of karma. Wealthy believers feel they are being rewarded for past-life virtue, and the opposite is also true. Members of scheduled castes may accept discrimination if they attribute their suffering to karmic debt.

Psychological Dependence

Brickyards and quarries are particularly brutal places for bonded laborers to work. Employers there often employ gunmen to guard their workers during the day, and they lock people in at night to prevent escape. However, this might not be necessary. Fatigue and malnutrition decrease motivation, so oppressed people tend to become compliant. Some laborers also become psychologically dependent on their captors because they know the bosses will give them a little food and a place to sleep. They may believe that bonded labor is preferable to the unknown.

money and no food, this equates to a death sentence. Arson and gang rape are also used to subjugate rebels.

Caste discrimination and debt slavery are closely interwoven. In recent years, legislation has been enacted to help counter discrimination against scheduled castes. However, laws are not always enforced. Human rights activists from Anti-Slavery International charge that authorities throughout South Asia often refuse to free debt slaves because of caste discrimination.

A dalit used a bicycle to pull materials
through the streets of New Delhi, India, in 2001.

Young Indian girls are deported from Saudi Arabia, where they had been coerced into prostitution and begging.

KIDS FOR SALE IN THE MIDDLE EAST

Slavery has a long history in the Middle East. It was not outlawed in Saudi Arabia and Yemen until 1962. Enforcement of antislavery laws is often inadequate, so the practice is still widespread throughout the area. There is money in this oil-rich region, and job seekers from nations throughout Asia flock there in the hope of a better life. Not all of them find it.

One common trait among exploiters is the tendency to prey on foreigners, and the Middle East is no exception. Women who go there looking for work can end up as sex slaves or captive housekeepers. Construction workers who want to send money home might find themselves behind razor wire at a job site. Children are not overlooked, for they too have value on the open market.

UNWILLING CHILD BRIDES

Women generally have low status throughout the Middle East. They must obey fathers and husbands, and widows traditionally defer to their adult sons. Saudi law allows fathers to force daughters into arranged marriages, often with older men who can afford to pay substantial dowries. In Middle Eastern culture, a dowry is a payment given to the bride's family by the husband. The dowry system induces poor men to let their

Child Brides

In 2009, a 12-year-old wife died in childbirth in Yemen, igniting a controversy about the age of brides in Muslim countries. Older men in Africa and the Middle East routinely marry girls as young as nine years old. Early pregnancies can be fatal because an adolescent's pelvis might not be wide enough to allow a baby through during delivery. Girls who survive may be left with fistulas, which are holes torn between the vagina and the rectum or bladder.

daughters marry as early as possible to obtain the payment. Most child brides are between seven and nine years old, but some are younger.

In Saudi Arabia, there is no minimum legal age for marriage. Ahmad al-Muabi, a Saudi marriage official, explained that baby girls as young as one year old can be married as long as the husband does not try to have sex with them until they reach puberty. Many husbands do not wait that long, believing that a girl of eight or nine years old is ready for sex.

Because women have few rights in Saudi Arabia, mothers of child brides cannot help their daughters. In April 2009, one mother from the city of Unaiza went to court in an attempt to annul the marriage of her eight-year-old daughter. The young girl's impoverished father had arranged her marriage to a 60-year-old man to pay off debts. The court ruled against the mother because she was not the child's legal guardian. In that country, fathers are the sole legal guardians of their children. Because of the controversy, this child bride remained with her parents for a few more years. She is still bound by her marriage contract and will be sent to live with her husband when she is a little older. The judge ruled that she can file for divorce once she reaches

Eleven-year-old Anita, right, and sixteen-year-old Birbal were married in India in 2006, despite laws prohibiting child marriage.

puberty. This case attracted national attention, resulting in the Saudi government promising to regulate, but not abolish, early marriages.

CHILD CAMEL JOCKEYS

Camel racing is a popular sport in the Middle East. Small children have worked as camel jockeys for hundreds of years, but camel racing has changed. The oil boom made sheikhs into billionaires, and what was once a pastime of nomads has become a big business. Prize camels can cost $1 million each—much more than the boys who ride them. Camel jockeys are easily replaced because they are worth only a few hundred dollars.

Life as a camel jockey is brutal. Camel jockeys are slaves who work 18-hour days in the desert, where temperatures can reach 120 degrees Fahrenheit (49°C). Rolls of barbed wire surround the camps to keep workers trapped. The children are usually housed in the stables with the animals, and they are starved to keep their weights down. They are weighed daily and punished if they eat too much. Discipline is harsh, and most jockeys have scarred arms and backs from whippings. Boys are often sexually abused.

Camel jockeys are trafficked into the Middle East mainly from Pakistan, Bangladesh, India, and Sudan. Asian children are particularly prized because of their small sizes and high-pitched screams, which startle the camels into running faster. Traffickers kidnap some boys, but families sell others. This happened to young Saddam, a

The Riches of Camel Racing

Khamis Harib is a camel owner who has been enjoying the Dubai racing scene for 20 years. For the owners of the expensive racing camels, there is a lot to enjoy. On race day, the owners—most of them sheikhs—sip tea in shady tents and nibble on miniature English-style sandwiches. The prize list is extensive, including luxury cars, yachts, mansions, and millions of dollars in cash. "It's a big honor to win," Harib said. "It's very competitive. If you win, you get your name in the newspaper and on television. . . . Everybody comes to kiss you on the nose."[1]

Bangladeshi boy whose father traded him for money to buy liquor. Now Saddam is a camel jockey living in a tiny handmade shack on the sand in the United Arab Emirates.

Camel races are entertaining for the spectators, but they are terrifying for the jockeys. The children are little more than toddlers—some are as young as four. Some sob openly at the starting lines. Most jockeys are too young to be able to ride well, so their handlers tie them to the camels. Others wear helmets and body armor, but protective gear makes the desert heat even harder to bear.

Boys shriek and whip their camels wildly when the race begins, and the camels thunder down the track. If ropes break, tiny jockeys go down under the hooves of the 1,500-pound (680-kg) animals. In 2005, this happened to eight-year-old Pakistani jockey Shakil, whose abdomen was split open when a camel trampled him. Shakil survived because he was taken to a hospital, but injured jockeys are sometimes allowed to die.

USE OF CHILD JOCKEYS BANNED

On March 31, 2005, the United Arab Emirates banned the use of children as jockeys and since then has even paid reparations to many of them. Oman, Qatar, and Saudi Arabia have also banned the practice, but this has only driven it underground. Illicit races still use child jockeys, which is why cameras are prohibited at racetracks.

Hundreds of camel jockeys have been rescued, but they still face difficulties in their home countries. In 2005, doctors in Karachi, Pakistan, treated hundreds of repatriated camel jockeys for conditions ranging from infected saddle sores to serious spinal injuries. All of them were malnourished. "Children are given too little food," said rescued Pakistani camel jockey Sarfaz, age ten. "When there are no camel races, we are used for hard labour."[2]

The Rape of a Seven-Year-Old Camel Jockey

On August 24, 2004, seven-year-old camel jockey Nadeem was raped in a camp in Banyas near the town of Al-Ain in the United Arab Emirates. This boy was unusual among camel jockeys in that both his parents lived near the camp. Nadeem's father, Rashid, and his mother, known as Mother of Shakeel, took their injured son to the police station to report the crime. Although police officers noted that the child was bleeding, they chose not to do anything about it. Rich owners of racing camels have political power, and police do not dare oppose them or their minions.

Rashid then took his injured son to the hospital, but when the couple admitted their child was a camel jockey, the hospital refused him treatment. Human rights activist Ansar Burney of Pakistan reported the incident. His organization, the Ansar Burney Welfare Trust, is working to stop such atrocities.

Another problem is the language barrier. Some boys were trafficked as two-year-olds, and they no longer speak their native languages. So their families might be difficult to locate. In Pakistan, in order to prevent unscrupulous people from making false claims, authorities required DNA tests before they released children to families.

Not all stories of repatriation have happy endings. Aid workers have recognized some repatriated children back at Middle Eastern camel camps. "Now the same parents are once again selling the children to traffickers who are taking them back to the Middle East to participate in illegal camel races that still take place; or sending them to extremist run schools that take on the costs for the children's upbringing," said human rights activist Fahad Burney.[3]

In 2007, a number of former camel jockeys were found in these extremist-run schools, called madrassas. Children who require expensive medical care are more likely to be enrolled, as the schools

A Brave Reporter

In 2005, photojournalist Daoud Khan visited the United Arab Emirates and met some young captives at racetracks and camel camps. Khan risked arrest by taking pictures of children there. At one camp, he was told, "If a child dies, nobody cares. . . . If there are few camels, 20–25 in a race, no child may die. But if there are 40–50 camels together, they run into each other and hit each other and children fall and die under the camel. It's not a problem if the child gets hurt. But the camel should not have a scratch."[4]

Camel Jockeying: A Nomad Tradition

The Rashaida are an Arabic tribe who migrated to Sudan. It is a common practice for them to sell their young children as camel jockeys, and they depend upon this income. "Why has UNICEF called it slavery and trafficking?" a Rashaida chief asked.[6] These people consider the practice part of their culture.

will pay the bills. However, madrassas indoctrinate children with jihadist beliefs such as admiration for suicide bombers.

ROBOTIC JOCKEYS: A SOLUTION?

The solution to the problem of child camel jockeys may take the unlikely form of robotic jockeys. The Swiss-made robots weigh approximately 60 pounds (27 kg) and cost about $5,500. Operators race alongside the camels in SUVs using wireless joysticks to control the robotic jockeys. The joysticks enable operators to make the robots pull on the reins and whip the camels. Wealthy camel owners have begun to prefer this form of racing because the expensive robots are status symbols. The aim of the robotic program was to "improve the speed, the weight, the aerodynamics, to reach the ultimate goal of completely phasing out children used as jockeys," said Sheikh Abdullah bin Saud, a Qatari official.[5]

Human rights advocates hope robotic jockeys will reduce the demand for child jockeys in the Middle East.

Trafficking victims await questioning by officers of the United Nations after being picked up during a nightclub raid in Bosnia.

TRAFFICKING OF WOMEN

About 80 percent of trafficking victims are female. About 70 percent of them are sold as sex slaves or unwilling wives. The rest become captive laborers, often as cooks, housekeepers, and sweatshop seamstresses.

VULNERABILITY

Women are especially vulnerable for several reasons. Traffickers can easily intimidate women into obedience. Another factor that puts women at risk for trafficking is gender discrimination. In many parts of the world, women are considered second-class citizens. Women are traditionally taught to respect and obey men.

Currently women make up 40 percent of the world's workers, but they own 1 percent of the property. Gender discrimination also exists in the United States. Until President Barack Obama signed the Lilly Ledbetter Fair Pay Restoration Act on January 28, 2009, US employers could legally pay women less than men for the same work. The bill is also known as the "Equal Pay for Equal Work" law.

Traffickers particularly prize submissive women from male-dominated societies. Traffickers want compliant workers, not rebels who constantly fight back. If women are trafficked into traditionally patriarchal nations such as those of the Middle East or South Asia, it is difficult for them to escape and prosecute their kidnappers. Authorities in such cultures may not challenge a man's right to keep or transport women as he wishes.

Trafficking of Women from Moldova

Moldova is a small country in Eastern Europe that borders Romania and Ukraine. It was once part of the Union of Soviet Socialist Republics (USSR), but it gained independence after the USSR collapsed in 1991. Now it is one of the poorest countries in Europe. In August 2010, the average monthly salary in the country translated to approximately $250 in US currency. Many people have left to find work elsewhere, and as a result, approximately

Changing Views

The Coalition Against Trafficking in Women is a nongovernmental organization (NGO) that works to protect the human rights of females. The group focuses on the issue of sexual exploitation, whether through prostitution, bride selling, or pornography. Its philosophy is that all prostitution exploits women, even those women who are in the business by choice. The coalition aims to reduce the demand for purchased sex through education and legal penalties for pimps and johns—people who use prostitutes.

In most countries, pimps get rich while their prostituted victims go to jail. In 1999, Sweden passed a law changing that. This legislation shifted the blame for prostitution onto pimps and johns. Ten years later, Sweden had the lowest rate of human trafficking in Europe.

Gunilla Ekberg, the coalition's co-executive director, was instrumental in bringing about Sweden's progressive prostitution legislation. Ekberg said,

It is the perpetrators—the pimps, traffickers, and prostitution buyers—who should be criminalized. In Sweden, prostituted women and children are seen as victims of male violence who do not risk legal or other penalties. Instead, they have a right to assistance to escape prostitution.[1]

one-third of the nation's children are missing at least one parent. Whole communities depend on remittances, or money sent home by members working outside the country.

Organized crime is well established in Moldova. Corruption is widespread among police and government officials. In addition to guns and drugs, Moldovan criminals have added women to the commodities they traffic. "The most powerful pimps in Moldova are all former cops," says Ion Vizdoga, the Director of the Center for Prevention of Trafficking of Women in Chisinau, Moldova.[2] According to Vizdoga, these pimps are protected by high-ranking friends in the police force and the Ministry of the Interior.

It was once easy for traffickers to entice girls with fake job ads in newspapers, but people have become wary. Posters everywhere warn of these dangers, but criminals are clever and inventive. In a new strategy, traffickers have begun paying individual Moldovans to sell their own friends and relatives. A pretty girl will bring $500—a large sum in a country where the average worker would take two months to earn that amount. Pimps will resell girls for many times that price once they transport them outside the country.

Suspected prostitutes from Romania and Moldova await questioning in Bosnia in 2002.

Another new tactic is called happy trafficking. After the stress of a few years of forced sex slavery, a girl might not be as physically attractive as she once was. Pimps sometimes let a girl go if she can recruit her own replacement. She returns to her hometown, richly dressed and carrying cash. Her friends are impressed, and the girl offers to help them find jobs too. She might admit that she was a sex slave, but she makes the job sound glamorous and exciting. Or, she might make up stories about modeling or restaurant work. A new recruit does not find out she is becoming a slave until she is sold.

TRAFFICKING OF WOMEN IN ASIA

Women and girls are trafficked throughout Asia as laborers, street beggars, and mail-order brides, but most are destined for the sex trade. Commercial sex is a big business in Southeast Asia, where it makes up 2 to 14 percent of the Gross Domestic Product (GDP). Although it is illegal in most of the continent, in Asian cultures it is often accepted for men to visit prostitutes. According to the Monitoring AIDS Pandemic Network, about one-third of Asian men who have the opportunity to use prostitutes do so.

Impoverished villages throughout Asia depend on income from girls whose parents sell them into sex slavery. Some brothels even have business relationships with villages that regularly provide them with girls. These brothel owners pay deposits to parents with attractive female babies with the understanding that they will return to pick up the girls when they reach approximately 12 years of age. Other Asian traffickers use deception or kidnapping to obtain girls.

Deceived into Slavery

Lena was a 19-year-old girl from a village in northern Moldova. She had been in a steady relationship with her boyfriend for a year and a half when he decided to sell her. Lena thought he was doing her a favor by arranging a waitress job for her in Portugal, but she ended up as a sex slave in Dubai. "I wanted money, and I was deceived," she admitted after her escape.[3]

The Coalition Against Trafficking in Women estimates that approximately 20 percent of Asian sex workers are trafficked, enslaved, or in prison. Trafficking victims in many nations face legal repercussions for prostitution. However, while the girls go to jail, police usually ignore the pimps who hold women captive and keep the money the women earn.

Child Sex Tourism

Some pedophiles avoid prosecution by traveling to Asian countries for sex with small children. Some of the children involved are rented out by their impoverished parents, while others are trafficking victims. One man to face charges was 61-year-old Wayne Nelson Corliss, who was sentenced on November 17, 2009, to 20 years in prison for molesting two young boys in Thailand. Corliss, who used to dress up as Santa Claus for parties, admitted to fondling boys who sat on "Santa's" lap.

Prostitutes walk the streets in 2007 in Rome, Italy.

Villagers in Tori Tokoli, Benin, say they are visited by traffickers who take advantage of their hopes to send their children away to school.

CHILD TRAFFICKING
IN AFRICA

Worldwide, volunteer groups, political committees, and nonprofit organizations join forces to combat the problem of poverty. However, the problem is a complex issue with many contributing factors. "If you add together war, environmental destruction, and economic crisis, you create the two main causes of slavery: poverty and violence," says Kevin Bales, president of Free the Slaves.[1]

All of these causes are present in Africa, which is still struggling in the aftermath of colonialism. Historically, European nations have ruled much of Africa. In the 1400s, the Portuguese set up plantations in western Africa to grow sugar crops and trade in slaves. In the late 1800s, many European powers raced to claim and control parts of Africa. After World War II, many African nations became independent—some through peaceful means, and some through violent uprisings. However, these nations were dependent on European powers for many years, and some have experienced difficulty and instability as they seek to establish their own forms of government. The frequent wars in

Albinism in Africa

Human trafficking in Africa includes adults, and some of the victims are albinos. Albinism is a condition in which a person's body does not produce pigment, causing the person's hair and skin to be very light or white. In some parts of Africa, an albino baby is seen as a curse on the family.

Other people value albinos—but for sinister reasons. Some witch doctors claim that potions using albino blood and body parts bring good luck. As such, albinos become targets for trafficking. In August 2010, a Kenyan man in Tanzania pled guilty to trafficking, intending to sell a captured albino man to a witch doctor. He was sentenced to 17 years in prison.

Africa bring lawlessness in their wake, allowing the strong to enslave the weak. If authorities are corrupt, slaves have little chance of escape. They cannot turn to police and government officials for help if slaveholders have already paid off the authorities.

Children are perhaps the most vulnerable slaves of all. Throughout Africa, they are captive fishermen, sex slaves, farm workers, and soldiers. Girls are forced to marry at young ages. But there are reasons for hope. African nations are responding to international

Population, Famine, and Slavery

In the 1960s and 1970s, the human population was burgeoning. Governments warned of impending global famine, and agricultural experts responded by supplying the developing world with pesticides and high-yield grains. The resulting increase in food production, called the green revolution, staved off famine for a time. Such a miracle is unlikely to be repeated.

Disease and food supplies naturally limit populations, keeping populations in balance with their environment. When well-meaning aid workers brought modern farming and vaccinations—but not contraceptives—to the developing world, this balance was thrown off. The global population quickly doubled. Despite the new technology, feeding everyone became a problem again.

Most overpopulation is occurring in developing nations, and people are suffering because of it. In dry sub-Saharan Africa, women cut trees for firewood, and animals overgraze the land. The land is damaged and not suitable for crops. Millions of people leave their ancestral lands for slums on the outskirts of cities. Hungry and powerless people can be desperate—and this makes them vulnerable to traffickers.

pressure to enforce antislavery laws. Consumers are gaining awareness of slavery used to produce some of the products they buy. The war against slavery has not yet been won, but some enslaved workers are rescued, and some slaveholders are punished.

CHILD SLAVERY ON COCOA PLANTATIONS

Although Aly Diabate worked picking cocoa beans for many years, he has never tasted chocolate. "I don't know what chocolate is," he said.[2]

When Aly was 11 years old, a trafficker offered him what sounded like a good deal: a bicycle and $150 a year for farm work in the Ivory Coast. Aly knew that money would help his impoverished parents back in Mali. What he did not know was that daily beatings were part of the deal. The trafficker did not tell Aly that he would never be paid, although he would work 12-hour days. On the

Fair Trade Products Combat Slavery

Diamonds and chocolate may be tainted by slavery. Cocoa bean buyers mix together beans from numerous plantations, so consumers cannot always tell whether slaves produced their chocolate. People can support cocoa producers who treat their workers fairly by buying fair trade chocolate. This certification means the laborers were paid competitive market wages for their work.

"Blood diamonds" come from African mines. The crews that dig them often include children. Conditions are sometimes similar to those of slavery. Diamond diggers might earn only pennies a day. Consumers who want to make sure their jewelry is ethically sourced can buy from companies such as Brilliant Earth, which mines its diamonds in Canada. Fairly traded chocolate and diamonds do cost more, but that extra money is directed to improving the quality of the workers' lives.

cocoa plantation, Aly and the other slave boys lived on a diet of bananas and a rare yam. At night, they were locked up so they could not escape. They slept directly on the wooden floorboards, but they were afraid to complain. "We didn't cry, we didn't scream. We thought we had been sold, but we weren't sure," he later said.[3]

They discovered they were slaves when their master, Le Gros, pushed a boy to work faster. "I bought each of you for 25,000 francs (about $35)," Le Gros griped. "So you have to work harder to reimburse me."[4] Aly dreamed of escape, but he never attempted it. "I was afraid," he admitted. "I had seen others who tried to escape. When they tried they were severely beaten."[5]

One brave boy named Oumar Kone did try, but he was caught and punished. When Oumar ran away again, he saved them all. He made it to a Malian immigrant village, where he told his story. Soon police arrived at the plantation, and the children were freed. Le Gros, whose real name turned out to be Lenikpo Yeo, was jailed. For Aly, the best part was the 125,000 francs (approximately $180) the boss had to pay him. Aly made it back to his parents and bought himself a shiny new bicycle. Later, journalists

Young boys are returned from Abidjan, Ivory Coast, to their native Mali in 1998, after they were discovered working as slaves on the Ivory Coast's northern cocoa plantations.

told Aly that US kids spend as much per year on chocolate as he earned picking cocoa beans. Aly had no resentment. "I bless them because they are eating it," he said.[6]

Child Soldiers

Children are involved in conflicts all over the world, but the problem is especially serious in Africa. Militias recruit children because they are fearless fighters who obey orders without question. Child soldiers do not understand the

UNICEF is the United Nations Children's Fund. It is a nongovernmental organization that helps people in developing countries, especially mothers and their children. In war-torn regions, UNICEF works to free child soldiers and treat them in rehabilitation centers. When the children are ready, the organization helps them return to their homes.

The 1989 UN Convention on the Rights of the Child expresses the rights of children to health care, protection, and education. It also includes an optional protocol that bans the use of child soldiers. Nations that sign the agreement pledge to make sure all of their soldiers are at least 18 years old and that they all enlisted voluntarily. The agreement also requires nations to punish any group using children as combatants. More than 100 countries have signed the optional protocol.

risks, so they will carry out the most dangerous missions. Before battles, commanders often drug them with marijuana, alcohol, or amphetamines so they will not be afraid. Kids are sent to the front lines during attacks. Many die, but the militias abduct more to replace them.

Some children join militias voluntarily to escape poverty or abusive homes. However, soldiers abduct the majority of them. This is what happened to ten-year-old Arek Anyiel Deng—but she was not to become a soldier. She is from Darfur in the African nation of Sudan. Arek was caught up in a territorial conflict between her black African farming community and Arabic nomads from the north. On the terrifying day she was captured, mounted raiders called *Janjaweed* rode into her village, firing their guns. Villagers scattered and ran, but men on horses and camels ran them down. The raiders

Children are used as soldiers in many African nations, including Liberia, Burundi, Sierra Leone, Uganda, and the Democratic Republic of the Congo.

killed most of the men and older boys and captured children as young as seven. An Arabic man named Dudu Mahmout claimed Arek.

"He told me that I was his slave and I had to do all the work he told me to do," she recalled. "I had to look after cattle and goats, fetch him water and firewood, and work in the fields. . . . We were often beaten if we did not do the work properly."[7] When Arek was 12, Dudu Mahmout began having sex with her against her will. "I could not refuse, because I was a slave."[8]

She bore three of his children, whom she loves dearly. When a government-sponsored program returned her to her home in 2006, Arek brought the children with her. She had been a slave for 18 years.

These two boys were among child slave laborers who worked under inhumane conditions breaking granite for their kidnappers in Nigeria.

Luis Pablo Puac and four other children were returned to Guatemala City
after being rescued from baby traffickers in Costa Rica in 2004.

CENTRAL AMERICAN
BABIES FOR SALE

L atin America faces the same trafficking
issues that plague the rest of the world.
However, Central America has one problem that is
not common elsewhere: the trafficking of infants
for adoption. Because of its proximity to the United

States, Guatemala is a source country for adoptable infants. Parents put many of these infants up for adoption. But some of these babies were kidnapped or sold by their own families. The problem is complicated because adoption agencies end up with a mixture of legally and illegally relinquished infants. The agencies themselves might not know the difference because traffickers can falsify documents.

WHY ARE BABIES TRAFFICKED?

Couples from the United States are willing to pay adoption fees of up to $60,000 for a healthy baby. The money is intended to pay the birth mother's expenses and to cover legal fees. In the case of trafficked infants, most of the money goes to middlemen, who make a huge profit. The large sums involved have attracted the attention of organized criminals, and now babies are missing throughout Guatemala. Several have been found in the adoption system, but many others are already gone. They were adopted into families in

Why the Demand for Babies?

Some couples in the United States put off having children to focus on their careers. Women experience a decline in their fertility as they age, so some cannot become pregnant by the time they are ready to start families. Many wish to adopt, but in the United States there are a limited number of available babies. Many older children are available for adoption, but life in foster care frequently leaves them with behavioral problems. Couples want young infants, and Central America is a ready source of babies.

the United States, and it is not likely their birth parents will get them back.

One Stolen Baby

March 26, 2007, was the worst day of Ana Escobar's life. On that day, the young Guatemalan mother brought her baby, Esther Zumalita Rivas, with her to work. Armed men burst into Escobar's little shop. She believes the attack was not random—she was targeted on purpose. "Maybe it's because they saw I was vulnerable, all alone in the shoe store," Escobar said.[1] The men locked Escobar in a storage closet and stole a few pairs of shoes, but that was not the worst part. "When I got out, my daughter was gone," Escobar explained.[2]

Escobar reported the kidnapping to the police, but she did not stop searching for her baby. Over a period of 14 months, she visited orphanages, hospitals, and police stations. After a year, she was not even sure what Esther would look like, but Escobar remembered the curved shape of her baby's tiny pinkie fingers.

Escobar was not the only mother in Guatemala whose baby was gone. Other distraught parents were missing their infants too. They pressured their government to revamp the corrupt adoption system, and the legislature responded. The Adoption Council froze all adoptions in progress to review every case. Every child had to be taken to the council chambers for an individual hearing.

Escobar waited in the lobby. Every time a baby was carried past her, she scrutinized it. On the second day, she saw a little girl who was about the right age. The foster mother let Escobar hold the child for a moment. The little girl had curved pinkie fingers.

Mexican Doctors Arrested for Selling Babies

On November 4, 2009, three doctors, a nurse, and a receptionist at a Mexico City hospital were arrested for trafficking babies. The doctors told mothers that their babies had died, but they actually had sold the infants for $1,130 each. For an additional fee, the hospital even provided fake birth certificates to buyers. The scam was exposed when the hospital director's son discovered the scheme and informed one of the mothers.

Escobar told the prosecutors her story, and they ordered the baby girl to be brought back. This time, the foster mother dropped off the baby, saying she did not want her. This seemed suspicious, and investigators ordered additional DNA tests. The tests proved that Escobar was the birth mother, and she welcomed back her baby girl.

It turned out that a doctor had falsified a DNA test to make it look like another woman was the baby's mother. Authorities moved to arrest the two lawyers, the foster mother, and the corrupt doctor. All of the traffickers fled except the doctor, who bailed himself out of jail. He claimed he had lost the rubber stamp he used to approve DNA tests.

Escobar found her daughter just in time. In two more weeks, a couple from Indiana would have adopted Esther. They were devastated to learn they almost adopted a stolen baby. They also mourned the loss of the baby girl because they had become attached to her during the long adoption process.

Escobar is delighted to have her child back, but Esther shows signs that the traffickers abused her.

DNA Testing

DNA testing is also called DNA fingerprinting. Each person's DNA fingerprint is unique, just as regular fingerprints are. The DNA fingerprint pattern looks a lot like a bar code. Every band in the DNA fingerprint of a child will match a band in the DNA fingerprint of either the child's mother or father. Comparison of the DNA fingerprints reveals whether certain individuals are the biological parents of a baby.

"She will not take toys, and when you lift your hand as if to hit her, she cowers and runs away," Escobar said.[3] Esther is improving, though, and in her mother's care she is likely to make a full recovery.

Casa Quivira

Sandra Gonzalez and Clifford Phillips are a young couple with bright smiles that inspire people to trust them. They live in Antigua, Guatemala, where they run the Casa

Ana Escobar plays with her daughter, Esther, who was returned to her after 14 months of searching.

Quivira adoption center. On August 11, 2007, authorities raided the center and removed 46 babies. All of them allegedly had been stolen from their parents, a charge the couple denies. "We have demonstrated to the courts and all we are doing is legal and with the consent of the birthmothers of these children," Phillips wrote in a letter to adoptive parents.[4]

Surrogate Mothers or Baby Selling?

A 2007 investigation by the Dutch government revealed that some Guatemalan women admitted to getting pregnant to sell the babies. The mothers make approximately $300 for a newborn—a lot of money in a country in which half the residents live on $500 per year. Such women prefer this unofficial surrogate motherhood to working as household servants, which would earn them about the same amount of money annually.

The Guatemalan government was not convinced. "There were allegations presented by parents that stolen children were in that place," said Guillermo Castillo, the Guatemalan ambassador to the United States. "While most of the adopted children come to this country to loving, caring families, I have also witnessed women becoming wombs for rent to produce babies for adoption, stolen babies, false identities and misrepresentation. The children are not merchandise."[5]

The other side of this tragedy occurred in the United States, where adoptive families anguished over lost babies. The locations of individual babies were kept confidential, so families were not sure whether they would ever see them again. That happened to Michigan resident Nancy Moylan and her adopted Guatemalan daughter Lilly. Years prior, Moylan adopted Lilly from Casa Quivira. When Lilly was nine, they returned there together to adopt a little boy. They bonded with a baby they named Jack. "They hand you this baby and you fall in love instantly. The minute you hold him, is the minute you know he's your son and that he was always meant to be your son," Moylan said.[6]

Soon after the Moylans left, the government raided Casa Quivira. Officials took Jack along with the other 45 infants. The babies were placed in various foster homes and orphanages while investigators tried to sort out which of them may have been trafficked. Months passed while babies waited for homes.

Moylan was thrilled to discover that Jack was not one of the

Does a Ban on Birth Control Contribute to Trafficking?

Some Christian churches believe that birth control should not be practiced. This idea stems from a Bible story about the great flood. According to the story, God caused a great flood to drown all the people and animals on the planet, except for the ones on Noah's floating ark. After the flood was over, God told Noah, "Be fruitful and increase in number and fill the Earth."[7]

Some conservative Catholic and Evangelical churches interpret this passage as an instruction from God banning the use of birth control. Celina Figueredo, who runs a Paraguayan shelter for trafficking victims, thinks this ban contributes to trafficking. Figueredo said,

With birth control proscribed by the Catholic Church, it is common to find families of eight children all under 18, exacerbated by teenage pregnancies at the age of 13 or 14. Many of the families make the problem worse by making the children responsible for providing for the family. They have to go out onto the street and bring back money; it doesn't matter how. Often they get exploited so they can bring back money, or sometimes in exchange for goods, clothes, fruit or vegetables.[8]

trafficked babies. Despite that, getting him home would not be easy. In January 2008, she received a phone call saying that she could go to Guatemala and pick up her new son. However, when she got there, officials had a change of heart. "When I got on the plane, I was pulled off and they told me that there was a hold on Jack's passport and he was not leaving," Moylan wrote. "In the end, I left without him. It was a total heartbreak."[9]

In March 2008, Moylan was once again invited to pick up Jack. That time, her sister took the plane to Guatemala while Moylan stayed home to handle the phone calls with officials. Jack and his aunt were stopped at the airport, but with help from fellow passengers, immigration officials, and the US embassy, the plane finally took off with the baby on board. "Everyone clapped on the plane when they boarded!" Moylan wrote.[10]

Adoptive Parents Return Stolen Girl

In 2004, Mike and Kari Nyberg adopted Sei So, a four-year-old "orphan" Samoan girl. As the child learned English, she told them about her family. The Nybergs realized she was not an orphan at all. They took her back to Samoa, where they found her birth family. Sei So's parents had not intended to give up their daughter. Corrupt adoption agents told them she would attend school in the United States and then return home. The Nybergs adored their adopted daughter, but they returned Sei So to her family.

Aides display Guatemalan children who were rescued from child traffickers and returned to their families in 2005.

Shyima Hall was ten when a wealthy couple brought her from a poor village in Egypt to work as a domestic slave in their California home.

THERE IS STILL SLAVERY IN AMERICA

*I*n 2006, the US Department of State estimated that 14,500 to 17,500 people are trafficked into the United States each year. Native-born Americans—mostly runaway teenagers— are trafficked too. The FBI believes there are about

100,000 of them. Numbers are difficult to determine, because very few of them escape. Faces of the others look out from missing children's posters, and their families do not know whether they are alive or dead.

In the United States, about half the trafficking victims are women and children routed into sex slavery. Unpaid domestic servants account for another 25 percent of America's hidden slaves. The rest are divided among various occupations, such as agriculture, restaurant work, and labor in sweatshop factories.

American slavery is no longer about the color of a person's skin. Today's traffickers exploit people of their own race as quickly as they would any others. Slaveholders such as pimps can make vast amounts of money from their slaves.

How Cultural Taboos Influence Trafficking

Americans probably see slaves now and then—but they do not realize it. Money can be a taboo subject in US culture. It stops people from asking nosy questions, such as how much money someone makes, or what a friend pays her live-in maid. Sometimes such maids are paid nothing at all—especially if they are illegal immigrants.

The fact that people do not like to ask questions about money makes it easier for exploiters to take advantage of their victims. The only hope that some trafficking victims may ever have is a nosy neighbor. "Why are these migrant laborers crowded into a trailer with no running water?" the neighbor might ask. "Don't they get paid enough to afford a better place? Do they even get paid at all?" Questions such as these defy the taboo, but they just might uncover slaves hidden in plain sight.

An American Housewife Turned Slaveholder

Money was clearly a secondary motive for Sandra Bearden, a middle-class housewife from Laredo, Texas. Bearden was Mexican-born. With that as an angle, she easily convinced a Mexican family to let their daughter, Maria, live with her. Bearden's offer was one that Haitian restavèks would be familiar with: a nice home, routine chores, and schooling.

The reality was that Bearden made Maria work constantly, and the child never went to school. Starvation and beatings weakened the girl.

Commercial Sexual Exploitation of Children

The US government recognizes that children are being exploited sexually in the country in both local and international ways. For example, teens can be kidnapped in their own hometowns and forced into sex slavery. In addition, the growth of the Internet has greatly contributed to the distribution of child pornography around the globe.

The Exploited Child Unit within the National Center for Missing & Exploited Children (NCMEC) was established by the US Congress in 1996. The NCMEC estimates that in the United States, one in five girls and one in ten boys will be sexually abused before adulthood. However, the NCMEC recognizes that because of the secretive nature of abuse, statistics can be incomplete. The group encourages the public to learn the facts about the commercial exploitation of children, including the importance of parental supervision and education of potential victims. Tip lines have been set up for people to report abuse. US government agencies such as the Justice Department and the Postal Service work together to identify child predators and rescue children from sexual exploitation.

When Maria was not working, Bearden chained her in the yard with no food or water. No one saw the girl there behind the adobe privacy fence until a neighbor had to work on his roof. Maria could have died if that neighbor had not spotted her and called the police. The girl was lying on the ground, chained to a post with her hands tied behind her back. Her legs were shackled together, and she was dangerously dehydrated. When the police arrived, Maria had not eaten in four days, and she could not walk.

When Maria got out of the hospital, her parents came from Mexico. Instead of blaming Bearden, Maria's father blamed himself for letting his daughter enter into a bad situation. "We made a decision that we thought would be good for our child, and look what happened," her father said. "I made a mistake, truly, and this is all my fault."[1] Bearden was arrested in May 2001 and is serving a life sentence.

The situation had far-reaching effects. Another victim was Bearden's four-year-old son, who went to live with relatives when his mother was convicted. The little boy must have witnessed his mother's cruelty, even if she did not harm him directly. The situation could affect his emotional development.

Human trafficking and abuse are closely linked. Traffickers must control their victims, and they do so through physical or verbal abuse. Many psychologists have concluded that abuse is cyclical—that those who have been abused are at risk of continuing the cycle of violence.

Witnessing violence at home damages children psychologically, even if they are never abused themselves. Toddlers who witness abuse usually have developmental delays. They might walk and talk later than other babies. By grade school, these kids often have poor social skills. Some try to resolve problems by force, perhaps mimicking their parents. When they grow up, boys and girls from abusive homes are at risk of becoming abusers themselves.

The Bearden case makes even experts wonder about the psychology of slaveholders. Clearly any sane slaveholder, no matter how unprincipled, would realize that little work can be extracted from a slave who is too weak to walk. Bearden certainly received free labor from Maria, but that was only her initial motive. The situation became more complex than that. Bearden gradually gave in to her desire to exercise total control over another person until she turned into a criminal child abuser. As trafficking experts Kevin Bales and Ron Soodalter describe, "There seems to be a sort of intoxication that comes with acts of greater and greater violence and control."[2]

TRAFFICKED US CHILDREN

US children are also trafficked—in their own country or across the border into Mexico. Most end up as sex slaves because their pimps keep all the money they earn. People might imagine that

Sarah Khonaizan and her husband, Homaidan Al-Turki, both Saudi citizens living in Colorado, faced charges after allegedly keeping an Indonesian nanny as a virtual slave.

kids are trafficked only if they put themselves in dangerous situations, but this is not necessarily true. Traffickers might pick up their victims in the most ordinary places, such as playgrounds, malls, and even the victim's own driveway.

It is not difficult to imagine why an immigrant in a foreign land might stay with traffickers. The victim likely does not know anyone else, and he or she might not speak the local language. It is much more

Do Not Take Rides from Strangers

Fifteen-year-old "Kimberly" and her 14-year-old cousin "Carol" were walking to a fast-food restaurant in Toledo, Ohio. When it started to rain, a couple pulled up and offered them a ride. "My mom told me a million times, don't get into the car with strangers," Kimberly said after her escape. "But I thought I knew the guy."[3] The guy turned out to be a pimp known as "Daddy," who forced the girls into sex slavery. Each girl was told that if she did not cooperate, the other girl would be hurt. Their pimp took the girls to a truck stop one night to solicit customers. One trucker who saw the young girls called the police. The girls were eventually rescued.

difficult to see why US teens would remain with traffickers, especially in US cities. Some of them are locked up, but others—such as streetwalking sex workers—could escape. The reason they do not comes down to fear and dependence.

Traffickers have a system designed to create this fear and dependence. It begins with rapes and beatings. Later, teams of traffickers work together, taking turns depriving their captives of sleep. This makes the prisoners confused and disoriented. Threats to the victims' families complete the mistreatment, and vulnerable young people can become compliant.

Abducted from Her Own Driveway

In 2006, 15-year-old "Debbie" was in her Phoenix, Arizona, home with her mom and siblings. (In many cases of news reporting regarding human trafficking, the victim's name is changed for privacy.) The phone rang. It was her friend Bianca, who wanted to drop by for a visit. When Bianca arrived with two men, Debbie went outside to meet them. They talked for a few minutes, and then Bianca said they had to go. "So I went and I started to go give her a hug," Debbie later said. "And that's when she pushed me in the car."[4]

It might not seem like it, but Bianca was also a victim. As they all drove away, the men threatened to shoot Bianca if she did not help tie up Debbie. The ploy was a common one among traffickers, who sometimes use one girl to capture another.

Debbie was tortured and raped. Her captors used psychological control to terrify her into obeying. Men arrived at all hours and paid her captors to let them have sex with her. The traffickers treated her like a dog, forcing dog biscuits into her mouth and locking her in a kennel. This treatment continued for more than

Avoiding Abduction

Experts have offered advice and techniques for young people to avoid abduction. For example, people who walk to school should walk in pairs or groups. It is also a good idea to vary walking routes to keep them unpredictable.

Experts also agree that it is imperative to never get into a car with a stranger—no matter what the stranger says. Kidnappers might attempt to coax a potential victim into the car with a lie. If a kidnapper attempts to pull a person into a car, the victim should scream, kick, bite—whatever it takes to keep from going in the car. Kidnappers often try to coax their victims to come quietly, so that they do not attract attention. Kidnappers are likely to give up when their target makes a lot of noise.

40 days. The dehumanizing treatment affects the mind of a victim, who begins to feel worthless. That worthless feeling is created intentionally; it is part of the system to create fear and dependence.

Luckily, the police received a tip that Debbie was in a Phoenix apartment, and they went looking for her. She heard them calling her name, but she was so traumatized she could not answer. Finally an officer found her tied up and stuffed into a drawer.

As usual, the traffickers had studied their victim before abducting her. They not only knew where she lived, they also knew she had a 19-month-old niece she loved. They threatened to kill her family and burn the baby with battery acid if Debbie did not obey them. "After they told me that, I didn't care what happened to me as long as my family stayed alive," Debbie explained. "And that's pretty much what I had in my head. Staying there to keep my family alive."[5]

Maria Suarez spent 20 years in prison for her role in the murder of a man who bought her as a sex slave and held her captive for five years.

A group of slave laborers await identity check at a village police station after being rescued from a brick kiln in Northern China in 2007.

THE IMPACT OF
TRAFFICKING ON
SURVIVORS

rafficking can leave survivors with issues that last a lifetime. The trauma victims experience falls roughly into three categories: physical, psychological, and spiritual. Support for survivors must address all these needs.

Physical Problems

Traffickers rarely allow their victims access to medical care. This care is expensive, and it gives victims a chance to report captors. As a result, trafficking victims usually have a host of chronic problems, such as rotten teeth from poor nutrition and years without dentistry. On the rare occasions that traffickers do take a captive to a clinic, they usually have associates accompany the victim into the examination room. The associates are intimidating, and they ensure the victim keeps quiet.

Authorities routinely take trafficking victims to hospitals when they are freed. Few survivors escape unscathed, and many are severely abused. Facial traumas such as broken teeth are common among girls who were captives of violent pimps. Survivors frequently have serious injuries, such as stab wounds, unset broken bones, or brain damage from blows to the head.

Illegal Abortions

Brothel owners do not always provide their girls with contraceptives. When unwanted pregnancies occur, they are usually terminated illegally. These dangerous abortions can result in hemorrhage, a punctured or torn uterus, or infection, all of which can cause death. Afterward, girls may suffer chronic pelvic pain and become permanently infertile.

Trafficking victims usually suffer from one or more untreated infections. Some are potentially fatal, such as the respiratory disease tuberculosis (TB). Infected people cough, and TB spreads through the air when others inhale droplets of moisture containing the TB bacterium. People who are stressed, malnourished, or crowded are especially susceptible.

SEXUALLY TRANSMITTED INFECTIONS

Sex workers face the risk of contracting sexually transmitted infections (STIs). Pelvic inflammatory disease (PID) is an infection of the reproductive organs that can lead to permanent infertility. Diseases such as gonorrhea and chlamydia can cause PID if they are left untreated. These diseases are curable with antibiotics, but the victims usually do not have access to medical care. The human immunodeficiency virus (HIV), the virus that causes the acquired immunodeficiency syndrome

Locked in a Cage for Two Years

Somaly Mam is a trafficking survivor who now runs a shelter for freed Cambodian sex slaves. She has rescued more than 50 girls from their captors. In 2007, Mam freed a young prostitute who had been locked in a cage for two years. Trauma had made the rescued girl mentally ill. Mam explained, "A lot of them, when they arrive, have psychological problems . . . very big problems. . . . And they never have love by the people, by their parents."[1]

(AIDS), is the most serious STI because it is incurable and fatal.

Condoms reduce the risk of STIs, but some clients do not want to use them. While free prostitutes may insist on condom use, trafficked sex slaves do not have a choice. Pimps do not usually care whether girls or their clients become infected. Some even force girls with AIDS symptoms to keep taking customers.

PSYCHOLOGICAL PROBLEMS

Trafficking victims typically suffer from psychological problems,

Symptoms of AIDS

People infected with HIV might have no symptoms for a decade. However, they are at risk of spreading the virus. Sexual partners of infected people have the highest risk. Condoms greatly reduce the chance of spreading the infection, but they do not eliminate it. An HIV-positive person begins to show signs of AIDS when the immune system is too damaged to defend the body. Infections and cancers set in, and they are usually the cause of death.

Signs of AIDS differ between men and women. When an HIV-positive woman begins to progress to having AIDS, she often has recurrent vaginal yeast infections. Abnormal Pap smears (cervical cancer screenings) might occur, along with genital warts or other sores in the genital area.

Both men and women with AIDS experience rapid weight loss without dieting, especially if they receive no treatment. Other symptoms include fevers with night sweats, fatigue, diarrhea, swollen lymph glands, and white spots or other blemishes in the mouth.

None of these signs can prove that a person has AIDS. The only way to know for sure is to be tested. AIDS is spreading fastest among adolescents, and many of them do not know they are infected.

Somaly Mam, a former sex worker turned activist, attended a news conference on child prostitution in Berlin, Germany, in 2006.

including depression, suicidal feelings or actions, self-mutilation, and substance abuse. Post-traumatic stress disorder (PTSD) is also common among survivors. PTSD is a set of recurrent symptoms resulting from a traumatic event. Its symptoms include fearfulness, irritability, and flashbacks—intrusive memories of upsetting events.

Survivors sometimes internalize the feelings of contempt that traffickers had about them. This is especially common among women who were trafficked into sex slavery. Survivors might feel ashamed even though what they did was not by choice. Former sex slaves routinely face discrimination if they return home to communities that view being a prostitute as a disgrace—even if forced to become one. Human rights activists are working to counter this unfair perception by focusing on the true criminals: pimps and johns.

Victims of trafficking are affected socially and might have a difficult time relating to others after being freed. Freed trafficking victims who entered the United States illegally may be eligible for special visas, so they do not have to return to their native lands. Although this is a positive development, it leaves survivors adrift without the social network of family and friends they once had.

Mariama Oumarou cries while she tells of her experience as a child slave in Niger during the Voice of Victims special forum in 2001.

SPIRITUAL PROBLEMS

Traffickers all over the world take advantage of people's spiritual beliefs to force them into slavery. There are many examples. The idea of karmic debt is used throughout South Asia to oppress people of scheduled castes. The notion that it is a sin not to pay off debt is exploited to force honest people into debt bondage.

In recent years, another example has come to light: the use of black magic rituals to force African girls into prostitution. The black magic is a form

of voodoo called juju, and it exerts a tremendous
influence over the lives of people in West Africa and
Haiti. Traffickers can leverage it to control victims.

In 2004, a 19-year-old Nigerian girl named
Sara was enslaved by a juju ritual before traffickers
brought her to Britain. Sara was promised a job in
the United Kingdom, but she did not know that it
would be sex work. Before they left Nigeria, Sara's
trafficker took her to a juju priest, who promised to
perform a ritual for her protection. "He cut me with
a razor blade on my back and on my
breasts and took my blood. He cut my
hair from my head and also from my
armpits," Sara said.[2]

After the ritual, the juju priest
threatened her. He told her that
if she did not pay back her debt to
the traffickers, the magic he placed
upon her would kill her. Her soul
would be hurled into hell. "This is
a lethal combination of criminal
networks and so-called juju priests,"
said Dr. Michael Korzinski of the
Helen Bamber Foundation, a human
rights organization.[3] Some Nigerian

Guatemalan Trafficking Ring Uses Witch Doctors to Threaten Girls

On February 11, 2009, five members of one family were convicted of trafficking Guatemalan girls into Los Angeles for sex work using beatings and threats against their families. They also employed witch doctors to threaten the girls with curses. Gladys Vasquez Valenzuela, the woman in charge, received a 40-year prison sentence.

Half of Trafficking Victims Refuse to Prosecute

Freed trafficking victims are exhausted physically and emotionally. In their fragile state, they might not feel capable of facing their abusers in court. According to Jennifer Stanger, the former Media/Advocacy Director of the Coalition to Abolish Slavery and Trafficking (CAST) in Los Angeles, about half of CAST's clients choose not to cooperate in prosecutions of their traffickers.

girls believe so fully in the power of voodoo that they will continue to pay off their debts by mail, even after they are freed from brothels. The Helen Bamber Foundation has provided aid to more than 30 African women, who, like Sara, were magically cursed.

It is important that survivors receive whatever kind of spiritual counseling they need to be freed from guilt and fear. This may mean a visit to another voodoo priest to lift a curse. In Sara's case, the help she needed came in the form of a blessing by a Christian priest from the Church of England, arranged by the Helen Bamber Foundation. She is happier now because she believes that the priest's blessing freed her from the voodoo curse.

Tiep Ngo received a special visa for victims of human trafficking after being held as a slave in a Daewoosa clothing plant in American Samoa.

In Bangladesh, where trafficking is a concern, a group of children travels to school on a specially protected bus to guard against kidnapping.

SOLVING THE PROBLEM

Throughout history, communities have tended to arrange themselves into hierarchies, with low-ranking individuals having less wealth and fewer rights than those at the top. Slavery is just one extreme in a continuum of increasing exploitation of the weak. In most cultures, slavery is illegal, but the existence of an underpaid servant class is considered normal. Individuals must decide for themselves whether such social structures are ethical or not.

In most cultures, women, children, and poor men have the lowest social status. Predictably, these people make up the majority of trafficking victims. Programs that provide education and job opportunities to at-risk groups reduce their vulnerability to trafficking. However, a great deal of work remains to be done to bring awareness of human trafficking into the public eye. Societal attitudes toward marginalized groups do change over time.

Despite the challenges, there are many reasons to hope that human trafficking can be stopped. Laws almost everywhere ban the practice.

Common Traits among Victims

Thousands of people are trafficked into the United States each year. Experts have determined common signs among these victims. A person may be a victim of trafficking if he or she is:
- Unable to move or change jobs
- Living in a small space with many people or with an employer
- Sexually exploited
- Suffering from injuries or untreated illnesses
- Fearful around other people, especially his or her employer
- Unpaid or underpaid for his or her work.

Rescuers should not confront traffickers personally. Instead, call 911 or the Human Trafficking Hotline.

Microcredit Loans Help People in Developing Nations

Microcredit programs have been discussed as a potential way to combat human trafficking. The trafficking of humans often occurs in poor countries, so experts study economic solutions.

Microcredit or microfinance loan programs allow individuals to loan small amounts of money so poor people can start small businesses. Lenders can loan as little as $25, either at a low rate of interest or with no interest at all. Microcredit Web sites allow lenders to see photos of borrowers and read about what they plan to do with the money. For example, a lender might loan a woman money to buy a goat so she can sell the milk. Although not all loans are paid back, they do have a very high rate of repayment. Helping poor citizens become financially independent could help protect them from those who would take advantage of them.

Police know about the problem too, and many try to punish traffickers instead of their victims. Perhaps most inspiring are brave activists who risk their lives rescuing individual slaves.

US Anti-Trafficking Laws

In the United States, the worst trafficking problems exist in states such as California, Texas, New York, and Florida, which have large immigrant populations. The state of California made human trafficking a felony in 2006 and required traffickers to provide financial restitution to their victims. Other states have laws combating trafficking as well.

A federal law—the Victims of Violence and Trafficking Protection Act of 2000—combats trafficking and provides support for its victims. The act provides funding for victims' legal aid, shelter, and counseling. Additional initiatives to keep children in school and to provide small business loans are intended to address the economic causes of trafficking.

THE TIER SYSTEM

The Victims of Violence and Trafficking Protection Act of 2000 mandates the US State Department to rank nations on a tier system. The rankings are based on how well the country complies with the act's regulations to stop human trafficking. Tier 1 nations fully comply with the regulations. Tier 2 nations do not fully comply with the regulations, but are making a significant effort to combat human trafficking. Tier 3 nations face economic sanctions because they are seen as corrupt regimes that are making no effort to combat slavery. Nations that are at risk for being dropped to Tier 3 are placed on a watch list to give them time to comply before facing sanctions.

India Placed on Tier 2 Watch List

In June 2009, Secretary of State Hillary Clinton released a Trafficking in Persons Report that placed India on the Tier 2 watch list. "India is a source, destination, and transit country for men, women, and children trafficked for the purposes of forced labor and commercial sexual exploitation," Clinton wrote.[1]

Representative Velma Veloria testified before the Criminal Justice and Corrections Committee in Olympia, Washington, on January 28, 2003. The panel heard testimony on two bills relating to human trafficking.

In 2010, the United States was ranked on the tier system for the first time. It was ranked as a Tier 1 nation.

Global Anti-Trafficking Laws

The United Nations (UN) introduced the Protocol to Prevent, Suppress and Punish Trafficking in Persons on November 15, 2000. Nations that sign the treaty agree to work together to combat trafficking and aid victims through cooperation in regard to information exchange. The signatory nations also agree to promote initiatives that prevent and protect potential victims. As of October 2010, the protocol had 117 signatory nations, including problem countries such as the United States, Moldova, and Nigeria.

Educating Police about Trafficking

Police sometimes treat trafficking victims as criminals, not victims. When police arrest traffickers and their victims, the situation can be complicated because both might be breaking the law. Victims might be in the country illegally, or they could be engaging in prostitution or other crimes. Such victims often see themselves as criminals, like 12-year-old "Tonya" did. She was arrested for prostitution as a child, but she never realized that her pimp was the one at fault. Later, Tonya told volunteers at Shared Hope, an NGO that helps trafficked US kids, how this affected her:

> *I always felt like a criminal. I never felt like a victim at all. Victims don't do time in jail, they work on the healing process. I was a criminal because I spent time in jail. I definitely felt like nothing more than a criminal.* [2]

Police departments are increasingly aware that criminals might actually be trafficking victims, and they are taking action. In Las Vegas, Nevada, the Metropolitan Police Department now has a special vice unit that investigates underage prostitution. Similar units have been established in cities such as Oakland, Dallas, and Atlanta.

John Schools

Norma Hotaling was once a prostitute. That is how she knows how much prostitution can hurt the people who sell and buy sex. Hotaling is the founder of Standing Against Global Exploitation (SAGE), an NGO that introduced the idea of "john schools." San Francisco's First Offender Prostitution Program—or john school—was set up in 1995. Johns are people who hire prostitutes. John schools are not exactly voluntary. Men who attend them have been caught soliciting a real prostitute or an undercover police officer dressed as one. They have a choice: face prosecution or pay a $1,000 fine and attend a one-day class. Most choose to pay the fine and attend the class.

At john school, men learn about the risks of STIs and about legal consequences for buying sex. They also learn how frightening life as a streetwalker can be from former prostitutes such as "Kira." She tells them about girls who were raped and assaulted. "You guys think we really liked having sex with you, but we would lie to you just to get your money. . . . I hated you when I was out there," Kira told the men.[3]

The goal of john school is to reduce the demand for commercial sex, and it does. Men who attend the class are 30 percent less likely to be arrested for repeat offenses.

AARON COHEN: A MAN WHO RISKS HIS LIFE TO RESCUE SLAVES

Aaron Cohen is a brave activist who works to free slaves. Cohen travels to countries such

as Burma, Iraq, or Nicaragua and
boldly goes into their most dangerous
neighborhoods. He is there searching
for child sex slaves, and the mobsters
who own those kids can be ruthless.
Cohen enters brothels by pretending
to be a customer and then takes
pictures to document the presence
of children there. He returns later
with the local police or a paramilitary
unit, and they free the children.

Freeing slaves is extremely
dangerous. Criminals who get rich
selling kids for sex would like to
kill Cohen. They have tried to more than once.
Cohen has been poisoned, shot, and chased by both
criminals and corrupt foreign police.

The girls he rescues go to shelters, where they
receive food and an education. It saddens Cohen
that not all of them stay there. Some pimps addict
their sex workers to drugs, and not every freed slave
has the strength to stay clean. Cohen says,

> *I struggle. But I think it is why I'm successful at what I do
> because I wouldn't just go into a brothel looking for bad guys*

**Oakland Police Crack
Down on Pimps**

When Officer Jim Saleda
started with the Oak-
land Police Department,
underage prostitutes were
routinely arrested and
charged. Too often, the
pimps escaped. Now the
department has a vice
crime and child exploi-
tation unit. They rescue
young girls and charge
their pimps with human
trafficking. Saleda said,
"Now we treat [prosti-
tutes] as victims."[4]

and good guys. I go in thinking: "We're all interconnected, there's light in this pimp, there's light in this child who's in sex slavery, there's light in this bodyguard, this Mafia guy"; and when you look at the bright side, I think that's the key to a lot of things in life.[5]

ENDING THE PROBLEM

People who work to end slavery hope that it will become an unthinkable practice. Governments and NGOs are working together to put laws in place that will end human trafficking. In early 2010, President Obama declared January as National Slavery and Human Trafficking Prevention Month. He said,

> *The victims of modern slavery have many faces. They are men and women, adults and children. Yet, all are denied basic human dignity and freedom. . . . All too often suffering from horrible physical and sexual abuse, it is hard for them to imagine that there might be a place of refuge. We must join together as a Nation and global community to provide that safe haven. . . . The men, women, and children who have suffered this scourge can overcome the bonds of modern slavery, receive protection and justice, and successfully reclaim their rightful independence.[6]*

President Barack Obama declared January as National Slavery and Human Trafficking Prevention Month.

Timeline

1619	1862	1865
Slaves captured in Africa first arrive in the American colonies.	President Abraham Lincoln signs the Emancipation Proclamation, declaring slaves in rebel states to be free.	The Thirteenth Amendment to the US Constitution abolishes slavery in the United States.

1995	1995	1995
Pakistan passes additional Bonded Labor System Abolition Rules to find and aid bonded laborers.	San Francisco's First Offender Prostitution Program, or "john school," begins.	Child labor activist Iqbal Masih is murdered on April 16.

1962

Slavery is outlawed in Middle Eastern countries Saudi Arabia and Yemen.

1989

The United Nations adopts the Convention on the Rights of the Child, which contains an optional protocol banning child soldiers.

1992

Pakistan passes the Bonded Labor System Abolition Act, making debt slavery illegal in the country.

1995

On August 2, 72 Thai workers are freed from a Los Angeles, California, sweatshop.

2000

The United States passes the Victims of Violence and Trafficking Protection Act, a federal law intended to stop trafficking.

2000

The United Nations passes the Protocol to Prevent, Suppress and Punish Trafficking in Persons on November 15.

TIMELINE

2001

In May, Sandra Bearden is arrested and sentenced to life in prison for abusing a Mexican girl she used for labor.

2005

The United Arab Emirates bans the use of children as camel jockeys on March 31.

2006

California makes human trafficking a felony.

2009

US President Barack Obama signs the "Equal Pay for Equal Work" law on January 28.

2009

US Secretary of State Hillary Clinton places India on the Tier 2 watch list in June.

2009

On November 17, Wayne Nelson Corliss is sentenced to 20 years in prison for sex tourism in Thailand.

2007

Repatriated child camel jockeys are found in Pakistani madrassas, allegedly training as terrorists.

2007

On August 11, authorities raid the Casa Quivira adoption center in Guatemala and remove 46 babies allegedly stolen from their parents.

2009

An International Labour Conference report estimates there are 33,000 forced laborers in Amazon jungle camps.

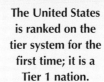

2010

President Barack Obama declares January to be National Slavery and Human Trafficking Prevention Month.

2010

The United States is ranked on the tier system for the first time; it is a Tier 1 nation.

Essential Facts

At Issue

❖ Experts estimate there are between 27 and 60 million enslaved people in the world today.

❖ Human trafficking is modern slavery. Victims are forced to work against their wills for the profit of another person. This slavery can take many forms, including sexual slavery, domestic work, and forced labor. It happens in nations around the world, including the United States.

❖ Poverty is linked to trafficking. People in overpopulated regions where resources are scarce are especially vulnerable to traffickers.

❖ Debt slavery, in which a person agrees to pay off a debt with labor, is a problem in many South Asian countries. Generations of workers are exploited as debt is handed from parents to children.

❖ Children are trafficked for many reasons, including sex slavery, for work as camel jockeys, or to be used as workers or soldiers. Babies are trafficked into the United States under the guise of adoption. Traffickers steal babies to collect adoption fees from adoptive parents.

❖ Trafficking victims face physical problems such as disease and injury. They also might face spiritual or psychological problems from years of abuse.

Critical Dates

1865
The Thirteenth Amendment to the US Constitution made slavery illegal in the United States. The US slave trade had begun in the early 1600s.

1990s
Pakistan passed legislation to make debt slavery illegal. Additional laws established committees to find and aid bonded laborers who still worked in slavery.

2000

The United Nations passed the Protocol to Prevent, Suppress and Punish Trafficking in Persons. Signatory nations agree to share information in an effort to end human trafficking.

2010

The United States ranked itself on its tier system, which ranks countries based on their efforts to combat human trafficking. The United States ranked as a Tier I nation, which means it fully complied with regulations set forth by the Victims of Violence and Trafficking Protection Act.

Quotes

"If you add together war, environmental destruction, and economic crisis, you create the two main causes of slavery: poverty and violence." —*Kevin Bales, president of Free the Slaves*

"It is the perpetrators—the pimps, traffickers, and prostitution buyers—who should be criminalized. In Sweden, prostituted women and children are seen as victims of male violence who do not risk legal or other penalties. Instead, they have a right to assistance to escape prostitution." —*Gunilla Ekberg, co-executive director of The Coalition Against Trafficking in Women*

"While most of the adopted children come to this country to loving, caring families, I have also witnessed women becoming wombs for rent to produce babies for adoption, stolen babies, false identities and misrepresentation. The children are not merchandise." —*Guillermo Castillo, Guatemalan ambassador to the United States*

GLOSSARY

abduct
    To kidnap or lead a person away illegally.

atrocities
    Appalling conditions, actions, or situations.

brothel
    A house of prostitution.

contraceptives
    Methods or items such as pills or condoms that are intended to prevent pregnancy.

corruption
    Dishonesty; moral depravity.

deception
    A trick or a plan to make someone believe a lie.

deportation
    The removal of an unlawful alien from a state or a country.

exploitation
    Using other people for personal gain.

illiterate
    Unable to read or write.

indoctrinate
    To instruct with a biased belief or point of view.

intimidation
    Inducement of fear.

pedophile
    An adult with an abnormal sexual attraction to children.

psychological
> Having to do with the mind.

relinquish
> To let go or release.

reparation
> Monetary compensation for an injury or wrong done.

repercussion
> A result of some event or action.

retaliation
> Revenge.

rudimentary
> Primitive, undeveloped, basic, or simple.

subjugate
> To enslave or make submissive.

susceptible
> Vulnerable.

unscrupulous
> Unprincipled and immoral.

ADDITIONAL RESOURCES

SELECTED BIBLIOGRAPHY

Bales, Kevin, and Ron Soodalter. *The Slave Next Door: Human Trafficking and Slavery in America Today.* Berkeley, CA: U of California P, 2009. Print.

Cohen, Aaron. *Slave Hunter: One Man's Global Quest to Free Victims of Human Trafficking.* New York: Simon Spotlight Entertainment, 2009. Print.

"Fact Sheet: Child Victims of Human Trafficking." *U.S. Department of Health and Human Services.* Administration for Children and Families, 17 Mar. 2009. Web.

Skinner, E. Benjamin. *A Crime So Monstrous: Face-to-Face with Modern-Day Slavery.* New York: Free Press, 2008. Print.

FURTHER READINGS

Bales, Kevin. *Understanding Global Slavery: A Reader.* Berkeley, CA: U of California P, 2005. Print.

Bales, Kevin, and Zoe Trodd, eds. *To Plead Our Own Cause: Personal Stories by Today's Slaves.* Ithaca, NY: Cornell UP, 2008. Print.

Batstone, David. *Not For Sale: The Return of the Global Slave Trade—And How We Can Fight It.* New York: HarperOne, 2010. Print.

Cullen-DuPont, Kathryn. *Human Trafficking.* New York: Facts on File, 2009. Print.

Simons, Rae. *Gender Danger: Survivors of Rape, Human Trafficking, and Honor Killings.* Philadelphia, PA: Mason Crest, 2009. Print.

WEB LINKS

To learn more about human trafficking, visit ABDO Publishing Company online at **www.abdopublishing.com**. Web sites about human trafficking are featured on our Book Links page. These links are routinely monitored and updated to provide the most current information available.

FOR MORE INFORMATION

For more information on this subject, contact or visit the following organizations:

Botto House/American Labor Museum
83 Norwood Street, Haledon, NJ 07508
973-595-7953
www.passaiccountynj.org/ParksHistorical/Historical_Attractions/
bottohouse.htm
This museum chronicles the history of child labor and the labor movement.

Gilder Lehrman Center for the Study of Slavery, Resistance, and Abolition at Yale University
Yale University
230 Prospect Street, New Haven, CT 06520-8206
203-432-3339
www.yale.edu/glc/index.htm
The center is committed to the study of slavery, its effects, and its role in the modern world. The center offers lectures, workshops, and access to historical documents.

Source Notes

Chapter 1. Trafficking Is Modern Slavery
1. E. Benjamin Skinner. *A Crime so Monstrous: Face-to-Face with Modern-Day Slavery*. New York: Free Press, 2008. Print. 280.
2. Lisa Rein. "Mystery of Va.'s First Slaves Is Unlocked 400 Years Later." *The Washington Post*. The Washington Post Company, 3 Sept. 2006. Web. 3 Aug. 2010.
3. Edward Boyer. "Sweatshop Exhibit Revives Painful Memories." *Los Angeles Times*. Los Angeles Times, 24 Jan. 2000. Web. 3 Aug. 2010.
4. Michael Smith and David Voreacos. "Slaves in Amazon Forced to Make Material Used in Cars." *Bloomberg*. Bloomberg L.P., 2 Nov. 2006. Web. 3 Aug. 2010.
5. Kevin G. Hall. "Slavery exists out of sight in Brazil." *Mongabay.com*. Knight Ridder Newspapers, 5 Sept. 2004. Web. 3 Aug. 2010.

Chapter 2. Debt Slavery in South Asia
1. Jonathon Silvers. "Child Labor in Pakistan." *The Atlantic*. The Atlantic Monthly Group, Feb. 1996. Web. 3 Aug. 2010.
2. Ibid.
3. Ibid.

Chapter 3. Kids for Sale in the Middle East
1. Ron Gluckman. "Death in Dubai." *Ron Gluckman's roving reporter pages*. N.p., 1992. Web. 3 Aug. 2010.
2. Jan McGirk. "Ban on Child Camel Jockeys Sends a Brutal Trade Underground." *The Independent*. independent.co.uk, 29 Apr. 2005. Web. 3 Aug. 2010.
3. "Rescued child camel jockeys handed over to extremist groups." *Ansar Burney Trust*. Ansar Burney Trust, 15 Sept. 2007. Web. 3 Aug. 2010.
4. Daoud Khan. "Riding for Their Lives." *New Internationalist magazine*. N.p., 1 July 2005. Web. 3 Aug. 2010.
5. Blake De Pastino. "Photo in the News: Robot Jockeys Race Camels in Qatar." *National Geographic News*. National Geographic Society, 15 July 2005. Web. 3 Aug. 2010.

6. "Sudan: Child camel jockeys return home." *IRIN*. IRIN, 14 Nov. 2009. Web. 3 Aug. 2010.

Chapter 4. Trafficking of Women
1. "Abolishing Prostitution: The Swedish Solution: An Interview with Gunilla Ekberg." *Rain and Thunder* 41 (2008): N. pag. *Nopornnorthhampton.org*. 5 Mar. 2009. Web. 3 Aug. 2010.
2. William Finnegan. "The Countertraffickers." *The New Yorker*. Condé Nast Digital, 18 Nov. 2009. Web. 3 Aug. 2010.
3. Ibid.

Chapter 5. Child Trafficking in Africa
1. Kevin Bales and Becky Cornell. *Slavery Today*. Toronto: Groundwood, 2008. Print. 18.
2. Sudarsan Raghavan and Sumana Chatterjee. "A Taste of Slavery." *Knight Ridder Newspapers* 2001. *StopChocolateSlavery*. N.p., n.d. Web. 3 Aug. 2010.
3. Ibid.
4. Ibid.
5. Ibid.
6. Ibid.
7. Emma Lynch and Joseph Winter. "Audio Slideshow: Sudan Ex-Slave." *BBC*. BBC, 20 Mar. 2007. Web. 3 Aug. 2010.
8. Ibid.

Chapter 6. Central American Babies for Sale
1. Juan Carlos Llorca. "US couple almost adopted stolen Guatemalan baby." *Boston.com*. NY Times Co., 31 July 2008. Web. 4 Oct. 2010.
2. Juan Carlos Llorca. "Stolen Baby Found in Guatemalan Adoption System." *Welt Online*. Axel Springer AG, 24 July 2008. Web. 3 Aug. 2010.
3. Ibid.

Source Notes Continued

4. Marney Rich Keenan. "Guatemala's crackdown on adoptions leaves Michigan families with broken hearts." *The Detroit News* 11 Mar. 2007. *Pound Pup Legacy*. Pound Pup Legacy, n.d. Web. 3 Aug. 2010.

5. Ibid.

6. Ibid.

7. *The Holy Bible: New International Version.* "Genesis 9:1." *Zondervan Bible Search.* International Bible Society, n.d. Web. 4 Oct. 2010.

8. Andy Footner. "Tri-border Area of Argentina, Brazil, and Paraguay Sees a Rise in Human Trafficking." *Humantrafficking.org.* Academy for Educational Development, 29 Jan. 2008. Web. 3 Aug. 2010.

9. Nancy Moylan. "Re. Guatemalan adoptions." E-mail to the author. 30 Nov. 2009.

10. Nancy Moylan. "Re. Guatemalan adoptions." E-mail to the author. 1 Dec. 2009.

Chapter 7. There Is Still Slavery in America

1. Kevin Bales and Ron Soodalter. *The Slave Next Door: Human Trafficking and Slavery in America Today.* Berkeley, CA: U of California P, 2009. Print. 5.

2. Ibid. 28.

3. "Innocence Lost: Trafficking in the U.S." Video. *ABC News.* ABC News Internet Ventures, 16 July 2008. Web. 3 Aug. 2010.

4. "Teen Girls' Stories of Sex Trafficking in U.S." *ABCNews/Primetime.* ABC News Internet Ventures, 9 Feb. 2006. Web. 3 Aug. 2010.

5. Ibid.

Chapter 8. The Impact of Trafficking on Survivors

1. Dan Rivers. "Girl, 6, embodies Cambodia's sex industry." *CNNWorld.* Cable News Network, 26 Jan. 2007. Web. 4 Oct. 2010.

2. Kevin Dowling and David Leppard. "African Girls Lured to Vice by Voodoo." *Times Online UK* 21 June 2009. *The Ross Institute Internet Archives.* Rick Ross, n.d. Web. 3 Aug. 2010.

3. Ibid.

Chapter 9. Solving the Problem

1. Arun Kumar. "India Not Doing Enough to Combat Modern Slavery." *Thaindian News*. Thaindian.com Company Limited, 17 June 2009. Web. 3 Aug. 2010.

2. "Domestic Minor Sex Trafficking National Fact Sheet." *Shared Hope International*. Shared Hope International, n.d. Web. 3 Aug. 2010.

3. "'John Schools': Can Men Who Hire Prostitutes Be Reformed?" *NOW on PBS*. JumpStart Productions, 30 May 2008. Web. 3 Aug. 2010.

4. Barry Bergman. "Human trafficking steps from the shadows." *UC Berkeley News*. UC Regents, 12 Mar. 2008. Web. 3 Aug. 2010.

5. Carole Cadwalladr. "'Women Have a Hard Time Accepting That I Spend My Life Looking for Underaged Sex Slaves.'" *Guardian.co.uk*. Guardian News and Media Limited, 22 Nov. 2009. Web. 3 Aug. 2010.

6. Barack H. Obama. "Presidential Papers, January 2010—Proclamation 8471—National Slavery and Human Trafficking Prevention Month, 2010." *World Book Advanced*. World Book, Inc., n.d. Web. 3 Aug. 2010.

INDEX

abortion, 77
AIDS, 78–79
albinism, 47
al-Muabi, Ahmad. *See* Muabi,
    Ahmad al-
American Civil War, 9
avoiding abduction, 73

Bearden, Sandra, 68–70
bin Saud, Abdullah, 36
birth control, 63
Bonded Labor System
    Abolition Act, 19
Bonded Labor System
    Abolition Rules, 19
Burney, Ansar, 34
Burney, Fahad, 35

camel jockeys, 31–36
Campos, Marcelo, 15
carpet factories, 20–24
Casa Quivira, 60–63
castes, 24–26, 82
Castillo, Guillermo, 62
child brides, 29–31
child soldiers, 48, 51–52
chocolate, 49, 51
Coalition Against Trafficking in
    Women, 40, 44
cocoa plantations, 49–51
Cohen, Aaron, 92–94
contraceptives, 48, 77
    See also birth control

debt bondage, 18–26
Deng, Arek Anyiel, 52–54
Diabate, Aly, 49–51

diamonds, 49
dowries, 29–30

early slave trade in America, 9
Ekberg, Gunilla, 40
Emancipation Proclamation, 9
Escobar, Ana, 58–60

fair trade products, 49
fistulas, 29

Gonzalez, Sandra, 60–61
green revolution, 48

happy trafficking, 42
Helen Bamber Foundation,
    83–84
HIV, 78, 79
Hotaling, Norma, 92

impacts of trafficking on
    survivors, 76–84
involuntary servitude, 7, 10

Janjaweed, 52
john schools, 92
juju, 83

karma, 24, 25, 82
Kone, Oumar, 50
Korzinski, Michael, 83

Le Gros. *See* Yeo, Lenikpo
Lilly Ledbetter Fair Pay
    Restoration Act, 39
Lincoln, Abraham, 9

madrassas, 35–36
Mahmout, Dudu, 53
Masih, Iqbal, 21
microcredit loans, 88
Moylan, Jack, 62–64
Moylan, Lilly, 62
Moylan, Nancy, 62–64
Muabi, Ahmad al-, 30

Narcisse, Williathe, 6–10
National Center for Missing &
    Exploited Children, 68
National Slavery and Human
    Trafficking Prevention
    Month, 94

Obama, Barack, 39, 94

Phillips, Clifford, 60–61
Pompee, Marie, 8, 9
Pompee, Willy, 8, 9
Pompee, Willy, Jr., 8, 9
post-traumatic stress disorder,
    80–81
poverty, 14, 46–47, 52
Prevention and Control
    of Human Trafficking
    Ordinance, 19
price of slaves, 14–15
Protocol to Prevent, Suppress
    and Punish Trafficking in
    Persons, 90
psychological dependence, 26

restavèks, 7–8, 68
Rivas, Esther Zumalita, 58–60
robotic camel jockeys, 36
Rolfe, John, 9

Saez, Emmanuel, 14
sex tourism, 44
sexually transmitted infections,
    9, 78–79
sheikhs, 31, 32, 36
slave trade in Africa, 9, 47
sweatshops, 14, 38, 67

taboos, 67
Thirteenth Amendment, 9
tier system, 89–90
trafficked babies, 30, 43,
    56–64
trafficking in the United States,
    66–74
trafficking of women, 38–44

UN Convention on the Rights
    of the Child, 52

Victims of Violence and
    Trafficking Protection Act of
    2000, 88–89
Vizdoga, Ion, 41

witch doctors, 47, 83
witnessing domestic violence,
    69, 70

Yeo, Lenikpo, 50

About the Author

Courtney Farrell is a full-time writer who has contributed to a dozen college-level Biology textbooks and has authored nine books for young people on social issues and historical events. She has a master's degree in zoology and is interested in conservation and sustainability issues. Farrell is certified as a designer and teacher of Permaculture, a type of organic agriculture. She lives with her family on a ranch in the mountains of Colorado.

Photo Credits

RaveenDran/AFP/Getty Images, cover; Marcus Bleasdale/VII/AP Images, 6; Gurinder Osan/AP Images, 13; Dar Yasin/AP Images, 17; Stringer/AP Images, 18, 97 (bottom); Emilio Morenatti/AP Images, 23; Manish Swarup/AP Images, 27; Sherwin Crasto/AP Images, 28; Prakash Hatvalne/AP Images, 32; Kamran Jebreili/AP Images, 37, 98 (top); Hidajet Delic/AP Images, 38, 42, 96; Andrew Medichini/AP Images, 45; Erick Christian Ahounou/AP Images, 46; Clement Ntaye/AP Images, 50; Adam Butler/AP Images, 53, 97 (top); George Osodi/AP Images, 55; Moises Castillo/AP Images, 56, 61, 65; Ric Francis/AP Images, 66, 75; Ed Andrieski/AP Images, 70; EyePress, File/AP Images, 76; Fritz Reiss/AP Images, 80; Themba Hadebe/AP Images, 82; Michael Stravato, File/AP Images, 85, 98 (bottom); Pavel Rahman/AP Images, 86; Louie Balukoff/AP Images, 90; Susan Walsh/AP Images, 95, 99